THE UNIVERSE LOVES YOU

*Let Go Of Your Fear,
Trust The Universe And
Manifest Unlimited Love,
Abundance And
Blessings*

Shaun Grant
& Sarah Grant

Get ready to feel so loved and supported by the universe that you are freed from any limitations that have held you back from living your best life.

Dedication

The Universe Loves You is dedicated to everyone who wants to experience true freedom. When you trust in the universe, follow your inner guidance, and surrender to the best life has to offer, you can experience true ease and peace. This book is for everyone who wants to live the most incredible life and manifest easily and effortlessly while embodying the love of the universe.

Contents

Everything your heart desires the universe desires for you. All you have to do is think, feel, take inspired action, and be open to receive. Allow the universe to manifest greater than you could ever imagine.

#TheUniverseLovesYou

Introduction

The universe loves you unconditionally, it really does. Everything you desire the universe desires for you. Ask, feel and expect what feels happiest to you. When you feel adored and supported by the universe, the most incredible things happen. We have seen this in countless people's lives we have worked with and our own.

In 2020, we had to trust the love and support of the universe more than ever. We lost our main source of income and this led us down a path of fear, stress, and doubt. To top that off the Covid-19 pandemic was bearing down on the world and shutting down every opportunity to come out of this struggle.

The hardest part during this time was keeping our minds from focusing on the worst. We turned on the news and it gave us more fear. We spoke to our neighbors and that provided more anxiety and worry. The fear and uncertainty was contagious.

There was only one power to turn to and that was the love and support of the universe. We chose to turn off the news, get off social media for a while, and started going within from guidance through meditation, and spending quiet time in nature and in prayer.

Moment by moment the universe gradually began to show us that everything was going to be alright. We were safe and protected. As we began to trust more and more, our faith got stronger. Although there were times we reverted back to fear, for the most part we were able to stand firm in our trust, belief, and expectation of the universe's goodness.

In being in vibrational harmony with the universe, we began to receive creative ideas from the Divine. We learned to believe in ourselves more than ever because we strongly believed in the power that was working through us and around us. This was a life-transforming lesson that we knew we needed to share with the world.

More money came from unexpected channels because we made God our source, we healed our deep-held fears and anxiety, and we bought the car of our dreams.

Now is a great time to move into trusting the universe, allowing it to guide you on your journey, and be open to receive all the abundance and love it wants to shower you with on a daily basis. Let go of your fears and release your worries, and get ready to step into your true power of trust and joy.

Our highest objective in writing this book is for you to know with complete belief and conviction that you are always loved and supported. With this outlook, you become unstoppable in following your dreams, staying emotionally and mentally healthy, and being confident in who you are. We hope this book transforms your life the way it did our lives by living and writing it.

Please note, throughout this book, we will use all-encompassing spiritual terms such as God, the Divine, and the Universe interchangeably.

This is in no way meant to offend anyone but it is in our experience relating to these expressions as symbols of unconditional love and well-being for all. Feel free to use what is most comfortable for you.

The universe has been waiting for this moment, to offer you all the wisdom and understanding you need to make the best of your life. Keep in mind it is not something you need to force, but rather allow the beauty of this Divine truth to come and bathe you in its universal love and support.

As Albert Einstein said, "The most important decision we make is whether we believe we live in a friendly or hostile universe." What do you believe? What you decide to believe will inevitably be your truth.

Who would you become if you believed that you were fully loved and supported by the universe?

#TheUniverseLovesYou

Who Would You Become?

**"Few experiences are more satisfying
than becoming someone we always
imagined we could be."**
Gina Greenlee

Every time your heart beats it represents an
expression of the universe's unconditional
love for you. Every time you take a breath, it is
an action that you are 100 percent supported
on your journey. How does that make you
feel? Do you feel like you could be a success in
anything? Would you go after your goals
without hesitation?

Who would you become if you let go of the
tight grip you have on your life and your
endeavors? Imagine if you could let go of
control and step into the universal rhythm
that would bless you in everything you did?
How much more joy could you experience if
you release the outcome of how things
unfold? Underneath all your control is this
underlying essence of peace and tranquility,

that is always available to you.

By letting go of control, you honor your emotions and in doing so, you open yourself up to your emotional guidance system, also know as your intuition. Intuition is your guiding light to your highest good and leads you to the best path you can take. Imagine if you could tap into this infinite power within you and follow the inspired action the universe gives to you?

The universe loves you more than you can ever know. It provides you with a place to keep you safe, food to nourish you, clothes to keep you warm, and transportation to get to where you need to go. God blesses you with a healthy body and mind, to take care of and nurture. The universe is always blessing you. Although this may look different to many people it comes from the same place of love.

We often take this for granted only focusing on what we don't have or what we need more of. These blessing go unconsciously recognized. When we come from a place of already feeling grateful for what we have, we are blessed with more. The constant search for feeling like we do not have enough creates an imbalance within and an absence of joy in our life. Start with the abundance that is available in your life and spend your time being thankful for its presence.

Feel The Love And Support The Universe Has For You

As you feel loved and supported you will begin to see how this positively affects your life. You will begin to feel good and complete with who you are right now. Take a moment to feel the love and support of the universe with each heartbeat and every breath. Take your time with this, the longer you are in this state of acceptance of universal love and support the more it benefits you.

Who would you become knowing you are already completely loved and supported? Maybe you would finish writing that book that you have been meaning to write? Maybe you move to a city that is more conducive to your career success? Or, maybe you would live your life with more motivation, energy, and vitality? All of these possibilities are available now when you comprehend the gift the universe gives to you every moment of existence.

One example for us would be having the courage, with universal love and support, to leave Los Angeles and move to Florida. In the eyes of others, it didn't seem like the best move for us but we trusted and intuitively knew that the universe's love was guiding us to the greatest version of ourselves.

This move taught us how to believe in ourselves, trust our hearts and always follow what matters to us. The blessings we received from stepping out on faith to move across the country are immeasurable. Each step, whenever it looked like it wasn't going to work out, the universe stepped in lovingly and offered us a perfect outcome.

The beauty about the universe, although its methods are sometimes hard to understand, is that it always has an expansive beneficial effect on whoever decides to place their faith in it. The universe always delivers in a better way than you can even imagine. Even if you can't see it now, it is inevitable you can feel the effects of its love and support later.

Repeat To Yourself Throughout The Day

I am loved and supported with every breath I take. I trust the universe and fearlessly follow my dreams.

The whole universe desires to see you win and win big. When you have faith that the world is on your side, you can experience the highest fulfillment.

#TheUniverseLovesYou

Universal Desire To Thrive

You are always meant to thrive and the best part is the universe is on your side each step of the way.

The universe is set up for you to thrive in all areas of your life. The whole universe desires to see you win and win big. When you have faith that the world is on your side, you can experience the highest fulfillment. This is a fundamental truth that will transform your life when you expect it and believe it to be true.

As Vadim Zeland wrote in his book, ***Reality Transurfing,*** "if it works out great and if it doesn't even better." What he is saying is you always have to expect the best because the universe is on your side every single time.

Recall a time in your life when it seemed like things were not working out for you. This could be a relationship ending that led you to find your soul mate, you leaving a job that allowed you to start your own business that brought you so much joy, or not being accepted at the school of your choice, only to realize there was a better option for you. All in all the universe has a master plan that is oftentimes beyond our understanding, yet we can see the full effects of this plan when we look back on how everything turned out.

Take a look at nature and how it inherently flourishes. The abundance of nature is always unlimited. You can see it in the plants, trees, flowers, oceans, and mountains. Nature's very essence is to become the greatest form of its self. This goes beyond what is physically visible because true abundance is the invisible energy that surrounds us, moves through us, and covers every aspect of the universe.

Just how the flowers bloom in spring or the acorn becomes a massive oak tree, you are also meant to thrive. The universe is set up for you to become the greatest version of yourself. Nature proves this every day of existence. We are not meant to stay small but to realize our highest potential and create an impact.

Victory in life has already been given to you before you even take any action. You were born unique and equipped with everything that you need to be exceptional. The power lies within you. You are more dynamic and capable of succeeding than you could ever imagine. The universe has given you power, love, and a strong mind to do whatever your heart truly desires.

There is a Divine blueprint for everybody's life and the universe holds the key. The Divine blueprint is taking all your gifts and talents and using them to the best of your ability to create positive change in the life of others. One of the universe's greatest desires is to guide you to the unfolding of this incredible, life-transforming journey. Say yes to the universe's love and support and the doors will open to endless joy and fulfillment.

The Divine wants to give you what you want for yourself. You can trust that the love of the universe will provide all of your needs in any shape or form that is required. Think about all the ways the universe has provided for you in your life. Remember those times when you didn't see a solution and then seemingly out of the blue a solution presented itself? What about the time when you knew something you wanted was right with all your heart and then the universe did the complete opposite and it turned out to be an even greater blessing than you could imagine?

The universe makes no mistakes and forever has our best interests at heart. Whether it's removing toxic people, giving you the exact amount of money to pay your rent, or providing a career opportunity to transform your life, the universe is always loving and supporting you.

The universe is love. God is love. When you accept that love is always supporting you, you tap into your unlimited nature. All you have to do is let go, surrender and have faith that all is working in your favor and helping you to thrive. It's time to open your heart to receive all the goodness of the universe.

Imagine what life feels like if you could move from moment to moment with not just the belief, but the knowing and awareness that the universe loves you, that it has your back and it is carving out the the very best path for your unique Divine expression. This is the truth of your existence.

We are spiritual beings having a human experience and what that means is that our very true nature is a hologram of the universe, made in the image of the universe which is spirit and spirit is everywhere.

Spirit can move to so many different places, to so many different avenues of life and we are connected to that very power. That universal power has everyone's best interest at heart.

Let's take an example of what this loving relationship with the universe would look like. Imagine that someone you trust with all your heart told you on a certain day you would be receiving a gift from them. Immediately you would accept this to be true. You accept this to be your reality and feel there is no need to even question the validity of it. You can trust that whatever this person tells you you're going to receive, they're going to provide it at the time you were told. This is a correlation to how the universe works in our lives. Although we do not know the exact time of manifestation, we do know that the universe works in perfect timing.

You can trust that the love of the universe will provide all of your needs in any shape or form. The universe is formless energy, a Divine substance that is able, willing, and generous enough to take the form of the very thing that you desire within your life. It's up to us to resonate at a high enough vibration to first accept it as truth, then allow this to unfold in our lives from moment to moment. We should always be open to the goodness and love that is the universe.

Expect The Best From The Universe

Take into account that the universe has your back and in having your back, it's willing to give you whatever you expect it to give you. The power comes in the expectation that you will undoubtedly get what you want.

When we align our beliefs and expectations with our highest truth and expression, we get what we expect in life. If you want to find love, give love to yourself, and expect love from the universe. If you want success, feel successful now, and expect it from the universe. Only expect to be, do and have the best life has to offer. The power is yours.

You can see what you are manifesting in the future by observing your predominant thoughts and feelings at the moment. We are always manifesting whatever we are vibrating at on the scale of consciousness.

#TheUniverseLovesYou

Gift Of Vibration

**"How you vibrate is what the universe echoes back to you in every moment."
Panache**

The universe works on energy which is then brought into form by vibrational frequency, also known as vibration. Your vibration, your thoughts, and feelings, are creating your reality. This is a universal law, whether you are conscious of it or not, it is always working.

David Hawkins was a scientist who created the scale of human consciousness to measure every vibration that can be felt. This scale has a measurement for every type of feeling we are emitting to the universe. From the lowest vibrations of guilt and shame to the highest vibrations of enlightenment, peace, joy, and everything in between. It's a spiritual way to determine what quality of life we are creating for ourselves.

Map of Consciousness

Developed by David R. Hawkins

The Map of Consciousness is based on a logarithmic
scale that spans from 0 to 1000.

Name of Level	Energetic "Frequency"	Associated Emotional State	View of Life
Enlightenment	700-1000	Ineffable	Is
Peace	600	Bliss	Perfect
Joy	540	Serenity	Complete
Love	500	Reverence	Benign
Reason	400	Understanding	Meaningful
Acceptance	350	Forgiveness	Harmonious
Willingness	310	Optimism	Hopeful
Neutrality	250	Trust	Satisfactory
Courage	200	Affirmation	Feasible
Pride	175	Scorn	Demanding
Anger	150	Hate	Antagoinstic
Desire	125	Craving	Disappointment
Fear	100	Anxiety	Frightening
Grief	75	Regret	Tragic
Apathy	50	Despair	Hopeless
Guilt	30	Blame	Evil
Shame	20	Humiliation	Miserable

This map of consciousness not only
determines our energetic frequency but our
predominant view of life. Fear, for example,

creates an emotional state of worry and anxiety. It also creates a state of being and point of view that is filled with despair and stress. If you are living in this state of dis-ease on a daily basis, your life will be filled with circumstances that create hopelessness, depression, and anxiety. For many, this is unconscious in nature. It isn't perceivable until we take the time to dive into ourselves to figure out the frequency we are vibrating at. All we need to do is look around us and see our life circumstances to determine what we are feeling.

Emotional Liberation - Feel And Release

In order to transmute emotions like fear, anger, and shame into love, it's important to embrace the feeling they produce. The more we resist the negative emotions the stronger they become and linger within us, only to be awakened when we are triggered by a circumstance that resonates with the emotion.

Take time to feel the emotions you have been resisting until you feel a lighter presence within yourself. This can be done through meditation or silent time. As you sit with the emotion, allow yourself to truly feel the anger, fear, anxiety, or any other emotion. Allow it to be present and give it permission to move through your body until it's ready to be released. Ask the universe to help you heal your subconscious mind of this emotion. The universe will help heal you when you ask for its guidance and support.

Over time a gentle peacefulness will come over you in order to be aware that the emotion has been cleared. You will no longer be triggered by this emotion. The more you feel all your emotions, the more you can attract positive outcomes into your life. Embrace acceptance of these emotions and this leads to a state of welcomed happiness and harmony.

In most cases, lower-scale vibrations are jumping points to higher-scale vibrations. We are often led in life to feel more anger to feel a greater sense of love, to feel shame to feel a greater sense of acceptance, and to feel guilt to experience a greater sense of reasoning.

No vibration, feeling, or emotion is ever bad, it is only the universe's plan in leading us to the highest potential within ourselves. The universe would like you to know what your future looks like at the moment. All you have to do is discover what your dominant thoughts and feelings are in the present moment. This is a master key to living the life the universe wants for you.

Where Are You Vibrating?

Take an honest look, what are you feeling day to day? Are you experiencing more of the lower vibrational frequencies or the higher ones? How can you experience more love, joy, and peace? Can you see yourself living harmoniously in a state of love and acceptance? By answering these questions, you will find out what you are manifesting more of now and in the future.

"The universe doesn't hear what you are saying. It only feels the vibration of what you are offering."
Abraham-Hicks

"The world is a great mirror. It reflects to you what you are. If you are loving, if you are friendly, if you are helpful, the world will prove to be loving and friendly and helpful in return. The world is what you are."

Thomas Dreier

The Mirror Reflection

Everything in your life is a mirror reflection of you. Your life is a movie and it's projecting outwardly what you believe to be true. You are the writer, director, and actor of your life.

The universe is mirroring your deepest thoughts, feelings, and convictions about life. The universe picks up everything that you are putting out from a mental and emotional standpoint. This is how the universe operates. It takes the thing that we place the most importance upon with our thoughts, feelings, and actions, and amplifies it to the degree of making it a physical manifestation in the out-picturing of our lives.

The universe works on consciousness and consciousness is all about your awareness. When it comes to the universe you have to ask yourself, what am I being aware of? What you are aware of is what will show up in your life. We can often find ourselves wondering why life is a certain way. Why do certain people show up? Why do certain things happen? There is a mirrored effect of each thought and feeling equivalent to everything that is showing up in our existence.

The way to truly know why what has manifested is to go within. Go within through meditation, go within through silence and ask your inner guidance, what thought and feeling caused this person, place, or thing to show up in my life? If it's something that you would like to change, you can ask what is the highest guidance that will allow me to transform this experience?

One of the most important things in understanding that the universe is a mirror is that we can change what is reflecting into the mirror. For instance, you wake up in the morning and you go into the bathroom and you have something on your face. You don't try and wipe it off in the mirror. You wipe it off of yourself and then in the reflection of the mirror the smudge is wiped off. Life works the exact same way.

If there are any issues or problems present in our lives, we don't physically try to rectify these issues, what we do is go within to our consciousness, our deep thoughts, feelings, and mental beliefs about life, and we find out what is being held there. We can transform the thought, the feeling behind it, and before long the out-picturing of that consciousness will shape itself to our new state of being and way of life.

The greatest paradox of life is what you see, feel, think about others is a direct reflection of yourself. When you judge someone, you reveal a part of yourself that needs love, acceptance, and healing.

There is nothing in this universe that is against you. Nothing is working that is keeping you from your desires. The only thing we need to do is search our inner thoughts and our deepest feelings because they control everything that shows up in our lives.

"By thinking, practicing, and focusing on the thoughts that empower us, we choose to live life on our terms. Whatever is absent from your life that you chose to manifest, ask yourself if any thoughts standing in the way of your realization. The Divine mind will always give you the clarity you need."

#TheUniverseLovesYou

Your Power To Create

The power to create lies within you, the person you are, is creating the reality you are living in.

We've been wired to create the lives that we desire the most. The Universe has equipped us with a powerful asset that determines the outcome of every moment. Although we are unable to control outcomes, we can control our thoughts which then influences the nature of our results.

Your mind is your universal power because you are connected to every aspect of space in the cosmos by it. Your individual mind is a holograph of the universal mind and whatever thoughts, enhanced with strong feeling and emotion, you add to it gets relayed to the universal Mind of God.

Once it reaches the universal Mind, a vibration of energy is sent throughout the universe, faster than the speed of light, to match itself. This happens all day, every moment of every existence. Each thought is relayed to the universal mind and seeks throughout the universe to find a match.

To simplify this process, let's liken it to placing a phone call. You think of who you would like to call, you experience the feeling or desire of making the call, and then you place it. Your call goes to the exact vibration, or person, you called out to and returns the vibration to you (the other person picks up).

Our thoughts are always bringing back to us our experiences, knowing this we can use it in our own lives to create the life that we choose. We should always be aware of where our focus is placed. If your desire is to manifest a successful business, it's important to place your attention on already having this business in thought as well as feeling.

In the beginning, sometimes it's easy to fall into the trap of being fearful and focusing unconsciously on not having the business yet.

However, with enough dedication to feeling like you are already a success and knowing that everything is going to work out, you can right this error very quickly.

Because our minds work in a way that magnifies what we place our attention upon, it's of great value that we use this to our advantage. We must be specific and give ourselves any stimulation that creates an image of the business or a positive feeling of the business. This is called the priming effect. You prime your mind to be so familiar with the thing you are desiring to manifest, that it creates a feeling of already having it.

A maxim to always be aware of in life is this, "Nothing can enter your life unless it enters your consciousness first." This means that you can receive nothing that you desire until it is rooted within your thinking and feeling first.

It's the things that feel most familiar that have the greatest opportunity to manifest in our lives. When we create the idea that it's a normal thing to have, any resistance surrounding it will dissolve. One other thing to be mindful of is not to force the process. When we observe nature and all of its workings, we notice that it moves with effortless ease and grace. Using our minds to create what we choose to have is exactly the same.

Through that realization, we come to the understanding that nothing ever has to be forced, but must be allowed to take its course at the universe's pace before it can manifest into our lives. Trust, have faith and know with complete conviction that what you desire is already yours and you're only waiting for its arrival, much like a tasty meal at your favorite restaurant.

Everything starts with the mind. The mind is the catalyst that controls how your cells react which then controls what you vibrate into the universe. Master the mind by mastering your thoughts and begin to use these thoughts to create the feeling that matches the very thing you want to have. From there, you can never lack anything.

The greatest most fulfilling task of everyone is to discover who they can become through the process of self-actualization.

#TheUniverseLovesYou

Self-Actualization Of You

The person you dream about becoming is self-actualizing one step at a time.

The universe in its vast expansion and unlimitedness is pure formless Divine energy, also known as love. What that love entails is that the universe is always working in your favor. It's always supporting you in ways that will enable you to continually progress and reach your highest potential and the self-actualization of your life.

In order for us to understand the dynamics of the universe and its power, we must know what its primary objective is for existing. The universe represents the unity that moves in complete, perfect harmony. Every action is precise and timed perfectly to coincide with every other action that moves within the universe. Within the universe, there are absolutely no mistakes whatsoever. It is pure Divine perfection that moves in direct correlation to a two-part catalyst.

The first part is self-actualization. The universe lives to know itself in as many forms as it chooses. Because its power is unlimited, endless forms are created out of this dynamic energy. It never uses force, but will incessantly operate to actualize the potential of every entity (or energy within it).

Self-actualization is the direct embodiment of your universal blueprint, it represents your soul's greatest plan for coming to this earth. As you align your body, mind, and spirit with the universe, self-actualization occurs naturally through listening to your intuition. You get the urge to spend more time in nature, start a new hobby or start journaling each morning.

Self-actualization is an ongoing Divine experience that unfolds every day of your life. Just as a seed naturally becomes a fruit or a caterpillar becomes a butterfly there is minimal effort involved.

It's your inherent nature to naturally self-actualize, and this can look different for each of us. Everyone will experience self-actualizing working in their lives, it can arise as a thought, feeling, through a dream, an event, or a meditation. Whether or not we can heal and evolve from it depends on what we decide to do with the experience.

One morning Shaun woke up and after a dream, he was saddened to realize that he had been physically abused at a young age by multiple adults. It was a memory after so many years that he had blocked out. Shaun was suppressing his right to have a high self-worth by telling himself it was okay what was done to him. He thought it was normal and he deserved it for not being able to do things the way the adults wanted it to be done.

Shaun misunderstood what they were asking of him and then he would be whipped with a belt or branch, punched in the face, or slapped because of it. Now many years later he realized that he was not treated properly and it affected who he was today.

This is the process of self-actualization presenting the truth as a means of healing and allowing him to become a healthier version of himself. Shaun could have avoided it and escaped it for many more years, but eventually, because of the universe's intent to exercise unconditional love and self-actualization, the same issue would have presented itself down the road. The universe wants us to heal those things that we have suppressed and be as happy as we possibly can be.

We often feel the urge to withdraw from our problems, but they are simply there to enable us to realize our highest potential. That's a wonderful way to look at your life in order to comprehend that you never have to be afraid of anything at any point and time. When we jump on board, we discover a Divine support system unlike anything else.

Each step of your journey, self-actualization unfolds. Contrary to what it appears to be like, self-actualization is not a straight line. In life there are twists, turns, steps forward, and steps back, but our alignment with the universe always ensures that self-actualization will move us forward.

The second part is love. A perfect love governs every movement within the beautiful universe we live in. This is where you come in and why it's so beneficial to understand why the universe loves and supports you so much.

So when we truly think of the concept of love, what comes to mind? Love is unselfish. Love is kind. Love is gentle. Love is faithful. Love is strong. Love is easeful. Love is peaceful. Love is dynamic. Love is everything and so is the universe. To allow this concept to work in our lives, we must understand that this truth is available for us now. It is available for us to, first and foremost, accept and to implement it in a way that changes and transformations are immediately felt.

Imagine a time in your life when it seemed like you kept attracting the same types of people, places, and things in a repetitive nature. At one point you may have even stopped and wondered why this is happening to me over and over again? What was unfolding was the presence of the universe's unconditional love and its dedication to teaching you a valuable lesson that seemed to elude your understanding through previous circumstances for you to actualize into your authentic self.

Although painful, universal love refused to allow you to proceed until the message was received. This is an important time to look at anything in your life that has turned into a pattern. Once you've discovered that pattern, take a moment to ask yourself, what message is the universe showing me through this experience? Once again, because of its unconditional love, it will give you all that you need to overcome it and succeed.

Everyone can be blessed when they align with the universe. What was once believed to be difficult is only a matter of commitment. A commitment to whatever the universe decides to move you towards. The beauty of it all is that you can be 100 percent certain that by committing, everything works out in your highest favor and you are fully loved and supported.

Life exists for you to enjoy it. Life exists in all of its entirety, for your pleasure and fulfillment. You begin to see synchronicities appear in your life and it seems as if things simply work out in your favor. This is what's meant to happen. This tells us, imminently, that the universe loves us unconditionally to the point of giving us all of the Divine tools needed to thrive within our lives.

There's a dynamic, as well as significant reason as to why self-actualization and love are available for us. The God force energy can do more in your life with your implementation of these Divine tools. These Divine tools are your unlimited ability to think, feel, be, act and evolve.

When we begin to operate these from a Divinely guided universal manner, the dice will always roll in our favor. Why? Because the universe's primary objective, once again, is to manifest unconditional love and self-actualization. Your Divine tools open the path to these objectives, but under one condition. You will never have more than enough than you can handle in order to make your life the very best it can be.

If you think back to a time when you experienced challenges, if you look closely within those challenges, you'll see unconditional love inherent in the situation. I recall a time when I had gone through some emotional struggles in college and had to return home to regroup and cultivate a greater state of being. At this time, I had no money, no direction, and no place to live. But, bit by bit there was one act of love after every challenge that ensued. What I realized afterward is, through all the seeming hardships and challenging growth, the universe was acting on its infallible principles with perfection. It helps to be consciously aware of these ever-present operative principles of the universe, but it's not needed.

How powerful is it to know that unconditional love and self-actualization have been working since the moment we set foot into this world? This truth reveals to us the enormity in which we are cared for every moment of our existence.

Repeat To Yourself Throughout The Day

The universe loves and supports me unconditionally in all that I am, do, and have.

I expect the universe to love and support me unconditionally in all that I am, do, and have.

I trust and expect the universe to love and support me unconditionally in all that I am, do, and have.

In order to know you are in balance, pay attention to how you feel. Do you feel at ease, centered, and at peace?

#TheUniverseLovesYou

Balance Creates Universal Support

The Universe Expresses Its Love For You Through An Incessant Seeking Of Balance

Balance is a state of peace, it's not being pulled too far to one side or the other of the emotional spectrum. It represents the greatest position of neutrality. Neutrality is being centered and allows us to operate from the greatest form of balance. The universe is always creating balance to keep us in alignment with the universal flow.

There is never a time when the universe is not supporting and loving you through all your growth, hardship, and evolution. The messages, lessons, and gifts are always available to you to help you on your journey.

It's up to you to not ignore them, look past the signs or get out of alignment with the flow of balance. The universe doesn't judge you and is always here to help you get back into your alignment with your true nature.

It's of great significance to be aware of what it truly means for us as the universe seeks incessant balance. It indicates that no matter what happens in our lives, we can trust the universe and trust it willingly to ensure that we will always come out on the beneficial side of everything if we are willing to take a moment, listen and be present with its leading.

The universe wants you to be in balance so that you can receive all your blessings. That is why it is always seeking balance because you are receptive to receiving the best in life when you are in balance. In order to know you are in balance, pay attention to how you feel. Do you feel grounded, centered, and at peace? Then you are in alignment with balance. If not, then it's important to get back into balance to receive all the universe has for you.

Reclaiming Your Balance

Some of the ideal ways to get back into balance are to slow down, spend time each day in silence or meditation, go out in nature and just be. Unplug from technology and step into the rhythm of mother earth. We need to balance all the rushing and doing energy with slowing down and resting energy.

"Balance is the key to everything. What we do, think, say, eat, feel, they all require awareness and through this awareness, we can grow."
Koi Fresco

There is an infinite number of moving parts within our universe that all move in different directions. Yet, through this immeasurable amount of activity, the universe, through it all is seeking to rebalance itself in alignment with love and self-actualization through every living thing, being, or energy that exists.

Only through the Divine design of infinite intelligence is it able to accomplish this since the beginning of time. Let's think about that for a moment. There are 7.7 billion people in the world and the universe has the power to rebalance each and every one of them with love and self-actualization. Now to give you an example in order for you to see how this has worked and is working in our life.

We bought a brand new 2021 luxury SUV that we were over the moon excited for. We dreamt of this car, it was on our vision board and we were obsessed with it. We were in Boca Raton had a nice meal and then went to the mall. We were going along having an absolutely wonderful day, little did we know that a utility truck smashed into the front of our brand new SUV only 5 days after we purchased it.

It wasn't until the next day that we discovered that someone had crashed into our vehicle and fled the scene. It was hit so badly that the paint was scraped off, it was dented ,and the whole front grill was broken.

We went from being overly excited to feeling angry, upset, and frustrated. Little did we know the universe was using this to return us to a centered state of balance. Because there was so much energy dedicated to obsessive attachment we had moved out of alignment with universal balance. Just imagine a pendulum swinging all the way to one side as far as it can go, what happens next? It has to swing the other direction with the exact same force. Keep in mind, this is where the universe begins its process of rebalancing itself.

Once the emotions were felt and cleared, we progressively begin to feel a sense of peace. This peace is another step because it's the first step in realigning with love and self-actualization. Through inner guidance, it offered us a solution to getting our SUV fixed one step at a time.

It's always one step at a time, because you have to remember that you are so loved by the universe, it never desires to put you in a position of overwhelm at any point and time. The universe only wants to help you. Our SUV was fixed and back to us within a week and looked like nothing happened.

From there, we experienced a sense of relief. With relief comes a deep sense of joy that often resembles stillness. In this stillness, the love and the vibration of realizing your greatest potential returns. Hence, the universe is back in balance. We were no longer in a state of obsession with our SUV but more a peaceful state of enjoyment.

This was just one case, but the beauty of the universe's true essence is that it has no limitations. It can always get done what it needs to get done, and right away too. As we've taken the time to dive deeper into this process, we see the evidence that we are always being helped on the deepest level and should never feel like a victim when we follow the universe's lead.

The universe even helps us tremendously if we set an intention every day to always agree with universal balance. This is a great way to expedite the process of getting back into alignment with love, harmony, and abundance.

It's best not to judge life because we don't always know what type of blessing the universe is bringing our way. Receiving from the universe is more about trusting what your heart feels as opposed to what your eyes see.

#TheUniverseLovesYou

Releasing Judgment

"Judging a person does not define who they are. It defines who are you."
Anonymous

There's a wonderful saying that goes, "If you'd like to be shut off from the true beauty of the universe, proceed with judgment." This gives us a specific look into the ramifications of judgment in our lives and the lives of others. But before we get into judgment, let's reiterate what love truly is.

Love accepts things as they are without a need to change them or make them better. Love does not look for better but understands that what is happening right now is most important. Love, ultimately is freedom. Judgment, on the other hand, is bondage.

So why is judgment associated with bondage? Well, it's through judgment that we become prisoners of the narrow mind. The narrow mind creates an attachment to a certain outcome of how things should be while blinding us to the truth of what they actually are. Judgment limits our perception by taking in only a portion of the infinite possibilities of life. When we judge we close ourselves off from all the beauty that surrounds us.

There is a Taoist story of an old farmer who had worked his crops for many years. One day his horse ran away. Upon hearing the news, his neighbors came to visit. "Such bad luck," they said sympathetically.
"Maybe," the farmer replied.

The next morning the horse returned, bringing with it three other wild horses. "How wonderful," the neighbors exclaimed.
"Maybe," replied the old man.

The following day, his son tried to ride one of the untamed horses, was thrown, and broke his leg. The neighbors again came to offer their sympathy for what they called his "misfortune."
"Maybe," answered the farmer.

The day after, military officials came to the village to draft young men into the army. Seeing that the son's leg was broken, they passed him by. The neighbors congratulated the farmer on how well things had turned out.

"Maybe," said the farmer.

This story enlightens us about the truth about judgment. It's best not to judge life because we don't always know what type of blessing the universe is bringing our way. Judgment alone could make us miss it if we are not open to what the universe is doing versus what it looks like. Receiving from the universe is more about trusting what your heart feels as opposed to what your eyes see.

In most cases, our judgment comes from our upbringing. We are taught to be a certain way and when that way of doing things has been stored within our way of thinking for so long it seems as if it's the only way to perceive reality. In some instances, the judgments that we have been taught can potentially help us to experience more of the joy in life, but for the most part, they hold us back.

(Shaun) Growing up in the deep south of Louisiana, some parts of the state that believed in judgments that hindered the expression of love. I can recall one transformative experience that showed me the power of love when it came to judgment.

Racism was one of the most prevalent things in the south and the most challenging thing about it was, it was often done behind the scenes. In one instance, I can remember meeting a fellow student from a small town in Northern Louisiana that was known for racial violence.

This young man, at the time, claimed to had never seen a black person before in his life except on television. My roommate and I didn't find out about it until later on, but we suspected something about how he behaved whenever he was around us.

Regardless, of his actions, we gave him the benefit of the doubt by taking the high road of love and acceptance. Every time we would naturally be nice and offer whatever we could to show kindness. And then one day, about midway into the second quarter of our first year, this young man begins to open up to us.

He started to smile back at us, knock on our door just to say high, or offer food if he had extra. We actually got so close to him that by the end of the middle of the next quarter, we were driving home from a night out of having a blast and he turned to me and my roommate and said, "I just want y'all to know, I love you guys. You are like two of the nicest people I've ever met and y'all should know that y'all are my brothers for life."

For the first time in my life, I was actually witnessing judgment being lifted and transmuted into love. It was a defining experience for all of our young lives.

This whole ordeal created a realization that judgments are taught not inherent. We are born with the ability to love and accept everything just as it is until we are instructed to do it differently. This story shows us that if we go back to the root of where judgment started in any situation, we can reverse it and free ourselves to feel all the love that is present.

Where in your life have you judged something so much that it feels like it's a reality? Truth is, the reality is only a projection of our own thoughts and often based on a dualistic nature. We are led to believe that life has to be this and that, either and or, right and wrong, good and bad. These concepts create separation between us and between the universe. They pride themselves on inferiority and superiority, and judgment is usually at the very core of it all. We do this the most with ourselves.

Judgment of the self is a judgment that has sometimes painful repercussions. In understanding how the universe works, we know that it functions as a mirror to our dominant thoughts and feelings about ourselves and life. Whenever we are struggling with something, we are likely submerged in judgment which is creating resistance to the very thing that is unfolding.

Releasing Judgment

Here's a statement you can say often to yourself whenever you are struggling with self-judgment or any kind of judgment,

"I honor, respect, accept, and love that what is happening is here to bless me in many ways. I make myself completely aware of the truth of what is unfolding at this moment."

By taking away the emotional charge and focus on resisting the thing, event, or situation, we neutralize it and create a higher awareness around it by honoring, loving, and accepting it as it is. It works in every situation, but the key is to always remain patient. Never rush the universe to create an outcome. Allow and receive what presents itself at the moment, and you will experience an endless measure of peace.

Judgment is not present to harm us in any way, but it is prevalent to enable us to see where we have misaligned ourselves with the love of the universe. When something arises in your life, pay attention to how you are feeling.

If judgment comes up, say the above statement to yourself until you become aware of the highest choice for you. When we can embrace judgment as the signpost that directs us to higher consciousness, we will inevitably feel and live in alignment with the universe's unconditional love and support.

Fear is an illusion that has no power unless we believe in it. Transform your life with the belief in love, not fear.

#TheUniverseLovesYou

Move Away From Your Fears And Into Complete Trust

"Everything you've ever wanted is on the other side of fear."
George Addair

Living in fear and worry is a common feeling that many of us feel on a moment-to-moment basis or from time to time. Fear is broadcasted in our media, online, in ads, and can be found everywhere. Fear is a paralyzing feeling that at times feels inescapable. The more we fear the more we experience fearful thoughts.

A worrying thought can drain our energy and entertain us for hours, days, or years of our life. Worrying is like hoping and praying for exactly what you don't want to happen. Fear, worry and anxiety come from a place of lacking trust in the universe. What we fear we draw to us.

Fearful thoughts are not true because they are only "what if" scenarios, we most likely will not experience. Unless we consistently think them over and over again while imbuing them with emotion, the fear could manifest itself. Since we create our reality with our thoughts and feelings, it's imperative to move away from our fears.

Fear is more of a compass that shows you the direction your thoughts are moving in. If you have thoughts of a fearful nature, there are likely conscious or unconscious fears you have not faced yet.

Love, Accepting, And Honoring Your Fears

You can help these to come to the surface by asking what do I fear the most? Sometimes it helps to meditate on questions like why am I so worried? Why am I anxious? What am I most afraid of?

Once you figure out what your fears are journal about what arises and how you can transmute them into love. Journaling allows you to recognize the trapped emotion and by the recognition, you begin the process of releasing it. In most cases, the fear is a part of yourself that you need to love, honor, and accept more.

A practical way of healing your fears is when a feeling of fear arises say, ***"I love, honor, and accept this fear for the value it brings to my life."*** By adding "for the value it brings to my life," it ensures that your subconscious mind is less likely to reject the suggestion and overcome the fear.

The fear is showing where you are out of alignment with the universe and love. Do this every time fear comes up and eventually you will find that those feelings of fear will dissipate from your consciousness. Remember what you resist persists and what you allow puts you in the now.

Trusting life allows us to move away from fear and worry and into the present moment. When we trust life, we can easily receive the blessings coming our way. Through the process of relaxing deeply into the moment and trusting life, ourselves, the universe, God, we can feel true freedom and in the flow with the beauty and adventure of life.

The Trust Meter

Jafree Ozwald puts so eloquently in his daily Enlightened Beings emails, the importance of trust in your life. The ability to trust the universe can be measured by using a trust meter. Your goal is to get to 100 percent trust in the universe each day. Check-in with yourself now and see how much you trust the universe? Are you at 20 percent? 50 percent? 100 percent? The more you trust the universe the easier the universe can deliver to you.

"You can easily create anything you want in life with trust. When you deeply trust all of your desires will manifest at the perfect time, they simply do."
Jafree Ozwald

Trust gives you peace of mind and allows you to be in harmony with the universe and alleviates your fear. As you discover trust you can take back your life and experience true ease and liberation.

It starts with taking a small step and knowing that every step you take is a perfect step in the right direction. So trust the adventurous journey you are on and let the dreams of your bigger story unfold.

When you are in
alignment with love, you
are in alignment with the
universe, and it can
provide you with the best
version of your life, all
because of love.

#TheUniverseLovesYou

Align With Love

"Be universal in your love, you will see the universe to be the picture of your own being."
Sri Chinmoy

When we think of the universe in any frame of mind, there is one thing, in particular, we must consider when it comes to its core nature. Although complex in design, the universe is always simplistic in approach. The point being, there are only two emotions to navigate when it comes to our lives, love and the opposite of love.

We all should have some idea of what love feels like and if we don't, just think of the love you may share for a child, parent, pet, or passion. That love will present a shining idea as it relates to what is being conveyed.

Another great option is to ask yourself the powerful question, "What does love feel like to me?" Just by asking that simple question, the universe will send you a thought which will create a feeling that describes love in its purest form. It's important to know that every sub-emotion is a dualistic companion of love. Although opposite, they still ultimately lead to love.

If you take an introspective look at your early life, there's a high possibility you may discover things that made you feel the opposite of love. We know, for ourselves, we experienced feeling a lot of anger and resentment. At first glance, it's easy to think that these sub-emotions are present to punish you, but what they really help in doing is moving you closer to love.

How many times have you seen someone go through some of the worst relationships for some time only to find their true love after those challenges? The only thing that ever changes is the desire for love becomes greater when we experience the opposite of it.

The same goes for prosperity. Wealth, prosperity, abundance, and money all resonate on the same vibration as love. You could even go as far as saying that they are forms of love. Most extremely wealthy individuals at some point in time have experienced extreme poverty. Poverty was only present to create a greater need for love.

This love is so prevalent that every time we move out of alignment with love, the universe alerts us through feelings. This is simple yet magnificently amazing because at every moment we are either feeling love or not feeling love. And if we are not feeling love, the universe leads us to the path of realignment with love. Much like the concept of balance, it is incessant, yet gentle when it guides us to our highest vibration, love.

How does it feel to know that all you ever need to do to live the life you choose to live is align yourself with love? That's it! From there, every action will be guided to result in an experience of love. The joy this brings is truly wonderful because it is so easy to implement.

Aligning With Love

When you get up in the morning ask the question, "Where would Divine love lead me today?" Sit and meditate on aligning with love and just allow the universe to work its brilliance.

The universe desires you to succeed, be fulfilled and experience love so it offers you freely the tools, knowledge, wisdom, and understanding to create your reality in a way that brings you endless joy.

It's as easy as understanding, "Am I in alignment with love or out of alignment with love?" Therein lies one of the greatest keys to a life well-lived. When you align with love, you align with the universe and all the joy it has for you.

That which we search for
is already within us, if we
attune our hearts and
minds to feel and see
what we are searching
for, it will come flowing
into our lives.

#TheUniverseLovesYou

Step Into The Flow Of Universal Blessings

"Going with the flow is responding to cues from the universe. When you go with the flow, you're surfing life force. It's about wakeful trust and total collaboration with what's showing up for you."
Danielle LaPorte

It's a widely held belief that you have to work extremely hard through blood, sweat, and tears to attain your goals. The obsession with achievement has caused burnout in countless amounts of people. However, the universe offers a more effective, as well as easier way of doing things. Instead of reaching for what you want to become or have, the universe empowers you to be the essence first of what you are trying to achieve, and then it brings it to you.

The reason this is a more favorable option of doing things is that it keeps us open to the infinite channels that allow our good to come to us. The universal flow works through a balance of giving and receiving, if we are continually charging forward in giving energy to our goals without taking the time to receive, we block the universe's opportunity to manifest our desires in a way that's best for us.

The universe can only give to us in a state of surrender. Surrender is peacefully letting go of controlling the outcome and stepping into universal flow. It's about allowing yourself to become who you choose to be, doing what you need to do by taking inspired action, and now you are patiently waiting for the arrival of your goal.

An inspired action is an action taken from the guidance of your intuition. It has a specific action taken to bring about a direct result that correlates to the universe's Divine plan for you. Inspired action comes from the heart, in alignment with feeling good, accompanied by enthusiasm and a desire to act. Even if inspired action doesn't seem logical, its objective is always of a greater purpose, so it's important to follow it.

Balance With Universal Rhythms

With the universal rhythms of life, there are times to work, times to rest, times to play. If you are guided to nurture yourself, make sure to take time to rest and meditate. If you are led to experience more adventure, get out and do something fun. The more you balance these cycles, the more open you can be to your intuition the more happiness you will feel.

The universe gives to you through the path of least resistance. This path is a path of peace and relaxation. It's difficult to receive the universe's blessing if we are emotionally unbalanced. To always be in the flow of the universe's gift, cultivate a state of inner peace.

The universe loves peace. To be in peace means to accept life exactly as it is, without the need, desire, or attachment to change it.

Peace comes from spending time with yourself, without interruption. Sit silently for five minutes to one hour and allow thoughts to come in without judgment, allow feelings to raise up without concern, and just embrace life as it is during this time.

"One of the best lessons you can learn in life is to master how to remain calm.
Catherine Pulsifer

A healthy mind flows with the rhythms of the universe. It also tries to be in perfect balance which creates a strong level of peace and calm. Your mind should be your greatest ally, not your worst enemy. By positioning our minds in a state of love we follow the universe's lead and prepare ourselves to live a life we can enjoy to the fullest.

The universal mind only knows peace, love, joy, harmony, and abundance. We should be impeccable with modeling our minds after core truths and the easiest way to start is to seek and connect with the Divine. If we are experiencing worry, stress, or anxiety we can calm our minds to match the universe's mindset by simply paying attention to our breathing.

Your breath determines the nature of your thoughts. If you are breathing out of harmony with the universe, you will inevitably create anxiety for yourself. This is a result of the body being under stress which makes the mind follow under stress as well.

Breath Of Life

Align your breath with the universe. With your breath, you can feel connected to the source of creation. You can feel the abundance of universal love flow through your body. With each breath, you can feel the serenity and love within you.

An effective breathing technique is the 4-7-8 method. Breathe in for 4 seconds, hold for 7 seconds and release for 8 seconds. This method of exhaling longer than you inhale reduces your stress levels, calms your mind, and improves your overall health. If you practice this for an extended period of time, you will notice your heightened ability to be in the moment and serenity within your body.

The balance that is created allows our mind to experience more clarity, tranquility, and alertness to the universal principals of peace, love, joy, harmony, and abundance. Peace of mind is a state of being any of us cannot afford to live without. It allows us to see things for exactly what they are which is ultimately always a blessing bestowed by the universe. The mind aligned with the universe knows that there is only one power and that power is love. This love creates harmony in our thoughts, our feelings, and our bodies.

When mind, body, and spirit are aligned with the universal mind, the mindset that is present is magnetic to all good things life has to offer. The most optimal way to create this mindset is meditation focused on a Divine connection with God. Because God is all things, it immediately tells our minds that all things are well and complimenting us along our life journey in the best possible way.

Letting go in this moment allows you to experience more of life, the beauty around you, and the opportunities just waiting to reveal themselves to you.

#TheUniverseLovesYou

Let Go Of Control And Surrender

There is a great power inside you that wants to give you everything you have ever dreamt of. All you have to do is surrender and let go of how you think it should show up.

Life has a beautiful way of working out when you let go and surrender to the Divine. Nature is an amazing example of how you can thrive and allow life to give to you. The more we get out of our head, release the ever-increasing need to control our lives, the more we can receive. It's the paradox of life. We think that we need to control, work so hard for everything we desire that we move away from a place of co-creating with the universe to one of manipulation and hard work.

When you surrender to ease and flow, you open your life to unlimited possibilities. Only when you are willing to surrender control can the universe step in and create Divine magic within your life. Although we have to be dedicated to doing our part with our thoughts, feelings, and inspired actions, the universe does the real work when it comes to giving us the life we choose.

Once we learn to cooperate with the universal rhythm, creating the life we choose becomes a simpler and sometimes easier task. Just like a river flowing downstream with a strong current, going with the current would be the easy, universally supportive way to reach your goal.

However, in life, many of us are going against the current, causing us to stagnate or make minimal progress. When we go against the universal rhythm, challenges and setbacks arise to slow us down. You can always tell if you are in alignment with the rhythm of the universe by how you feel. Your feelings are the direct connection to universal guidance.

If you find that you are unable to decipher what the universe is telling you, you can choose to simply surrender and be still. Much like the example of the river, if you were to step into it and be still it would naturally move you in the direction of the universal current. Life is no different. Sometimes all we need, instead of trying to control everything, is to be still and allow the universe to guide us on our next step of the journey.

Surrender To Miracles

Miracles happen to you, through you, and for you, every day. We are often unconscious of its unfolding because we are so used to it happening that we forget the amount of joy focusing on it can bring to our lives.

One of the greatest miracles in your body. If you take the time to sit for a few moments with your body and observe everything that is functioning within it, your mind will be blown. Questions like, "What keeps my heart beating, or my blood circulating, or my brain processing information will allow you to see a miraculous operation unfolding within you every second of the day." Another is how grass grows. This is a miracle that is often overlooked because it's unconsciously expected. But if we took the time to watch the grass grow day after day, we could see another miracle unfolding right before our eyes.

When it comes to miracles, it's in our best interest to see them all as great and wonderful as opposed to some being greater than others. Once we set the intention to notice the miracles in our lives, then we will begin to become acutely aware of those miracles happening in us, around us, and through us that have always been there. In doing so, our appreciation for the intricate creation of life becomes a world filled with awe and wonder.

Life may seem mundane at the moment. Nothing seems to be unfolding that would be all that exciting, yet, once you choose to surrender to miracles in your life, your attention is moved to discovering the many beautiful ones of great magnitude occurring right now. Surrender to miracles now and watch the magic unfold before your eyes.

Surrender To Divine Timing

Everything in the universe works in Divine time. The universe is perfect in its delivery of every manifestation. This allows us to trust that everything we are hoping and believing for will show up in our lives at the exact time it is supposed to show up.

By aligning with Divine timing, you instantly can create a deep state of peace within yourself, as well as patience. Knowing that everything happens in Divine timing, you can free yourself from worry and anxiety and surrender to the truth that everything works out for our very best.

Surrender To The Fear Of Change

There is one thing that can be considered forever constant when it comes to life, and that thing is change. Change is inevitable in absolutely everything. The only entity that is not subject to change is the Divine itself. This brings us to the importance of understanding the universe's inherent nature of the change which is also ever-functioning in our own lives.

It can be easy to fear change because in most cases, we crave the ease of comfort. But, change is truly a wonderful thing and that's where we need to place our focus. The Universe only changes things to transform them into something even more wonderful than it already is.

If you think about the changes that have occurred in your life or in nature, they all create a better existence for the person or thing being changed. Whether it be an oak tree that loses all of its leaves in winter only to blossom flowers upon its branches, or watching someone lose their job only to find the strength within themselves to create their own business. It all works out for the highest good.

Change is never something to be feared, but something to always be surrendered to. When we can accept this process unconditionally, and even move to the place of loving it, it all becomes less difficult to endure as it takes place.

Surrender To The Comparison Of Others

Although we are all connected through the universal concept of Oneness. We are all unique Divine expressions. No two people are alike in any sense, yet, we've often been taught to compare ourselves to others at the risk of diminishing our own value.

If we know nothing else, it benefits us tremendously to be aware that God treasures, adores, and loves us immeasurably. Not just that, the generous Divine being has given us individual gifts that are catered to our very own way of expressing them for the good of ourselves and humanity.

We are remarkable beings whose magnificence is awaiting our recognition and embrace. No one has the beautiful gifts that you have and it's time to start celebrating these gifts, as well as your very own uniqueness. You can start by surrendering to comparison with others and loving everything about you.

We only compare ourselves when we either feel insecure about our own individuality, or we are unaware of what it is for us. Comparison steals the joy that is always present ready to flow through you.

Instead of focusing on comparison, our focus should be on creating. When we make the shift, all of the energy that we lost out on being concerned with others, is then projected into our own singular purpose. Choose right now to give up the need to judge yourself by the lives of others and embrace your wonderful essence by surrendering to comparison of others once and for all.

Surrender To Your Belief In Scarcity

"There is only abundance in the mind of God." This is a timeless quote that enables us to understand that it would be impossible for the universe to lack anything at any time throughout its eternal existence.

How can we know this to be true? The evidence of universal abundance lies in everything, absolutely everything. From the ocean to the human body itself, abundance is a representation of the universe that is present for our benefit.

Scarcity is conditioning that denies the natural state of the universe, abundance. It's easy to fall victim to a scarcity consciousness when you're taught not to trust in the Divine.

Our most powerful insight comes from knowing that we always have the power to choose. Abundance or lack shows up by our decision to choose which one we will observe in our life. One choice has the opportunity to free your life of lack and scarcity forever.

By surrendering your belief in scarcity, you open your consciousness to abundance. In this surrender, your energy allows the universe to operate in its inherent nature of abundance removing any form of lack and scarcity present.

Repeat These Slowly With Feeling

I surrender to ease.
I surrender to the flow of life.
I surrender to the beauty of this moment.
I surrender to my unlimited potential.
I surrender to my soul joy.
I surrender to giving and receiving.
I surrender to what makes me happy.
I surrender to the universe's plan.
I surrender to the Divine.
I let go and relax.
I trust and know everything is working for me.
I surrender and let go.
I relax into the bliss of now.

No matter what is happening in the world, I can always feel peace.

I am free to do what I love.

My life is easy when I surrender to what is and deeply relax being me.

I surrender to universal guidance and am open to receive all my blessings.

The universe wants to give to you easily and effortlessly. Tap into what brings you joy and as you follow your bliss, more is given to you.

#TheUniverseLovesYou

Follow Your Joy

"Follow your bliss and the universe will open doors for you where there were only walls."
Joseph Campbell

The universe loves to give to you in easy and effortless ways. It's in your feelings of joy, love, acceptance, and peace that you are in alignment with the universe. This state allows the universe to give abundantly to you and shower you with its love. Our natural state is one of light-heartedness, one of joy and flow. The more we are grounded in acceptance, freedom, and love, the less we have to struggle.

How do you know when you are not in alignment with the universe, God, the source of life? When you feel fear, anger, resentment, worry, or anything that doesn't make you feel good. When in these unhappy and sometimes destructive states, we create more problems and painful experiences for ourselves. These negative states bring a downward spiral leaving you out of alignment with the flow and ease of life. In our fear, we feel powerless, we do not feel supported or loved. The ego likes to keep you wrapped in these negative thoughts and worries. Negative emotions take away your power and keep you from your desires. They lead you down the path of struggle, unease, and pain.

Your power is in your happiness, passion, and state of unconditional love. In these positive feelings, you are alignment with the universe and are showered with love and support.

Choose to move toward the feelings that make you feel good. The more you bathe in feelings of excitement, grace, and passion, the more you are in alignment with the greatest good for your life. You deserve to feel your best and feel supported.

Tune Into Universal Guidance

Intuition is a feeling. It feels like peace, ease, and sometimes joy. It's always going to reassure you that the action you are guided to take will always work out. To follow the lead of the universe and listen to your intuition, it's essential to start asking for guidance and listening for the answers. The answers can come to you in so many ways, such as a dream, a book you were led to read, a conversation, during your meditation or thought while driving to work.

Your intuition is forever guiding you to help you on your journey. Pay attention to the signs, the insights, and the direction to go in. When you move from a place of universal guidance you are one step closer to manifesting what you desire.

It is so helpful to know that at the core of your being is an abundant river of bliss flowing through you. You can tap into it at any time, as you quiet the mind chatter and open your heart to the peace within you. You will find it as you let go with ease and trust. The core of your being is always in alignment with the universe. It is your soul helping guide you on your journey. But for many of us, we get lost in our negative thoughts, criticisms of ourselves and others and feel a deep sense of fear that we try to hide. There is nothing to be afraid of when you align with God, the universe.

Joy has Divine magic written all over it. Joy possesses a lightness to it that when felt for extended periods, has the potential to open us up to soul qualities within our own being. Developing our soul qualities is one of the greatest purposes in our lives. We have come here to learn the soul qualities of acceptance, forgiveness, unconditional love, and compassion. As we evolve and grow more, our inner attributes shine through us.

When we are submerged in the joy the universe so willingly offers every moment of existence, our awareness is enhanced that sheds light on everything that is Divinely meant to help us reach our greatest potential. Because joy is one of the highest frequencies on the vibrational scale of consciousness, it is going to open the gateway to all inner qualities that enable us to see the love present in all things. We can say that joy is an accessing point that opens up one of the most powerful truths of our existence, we are infinite, eternal, unlimited beings primed for endless joy.

Opportunities are available all around you if you open your eyes and are willing to receive them. Let go of being attached to one particular outcome because the universe will bless you in many ways that you cannot quite anticipate.

What if you are missing out on all the beauty life has to offer because you are so focused on achieving one goal? What if the universe wants to give you something so much more than that one goal you have set your mind to? What if the universe wants to give you 100 times better than the goal you have, however, since you are so narrow-focused on that one goal you are missing all the other blessings trying to be given to you.

When we follow our creativity and passions, it can change as we embark on the journey of achieving it. Open to the possibilities unfolding before you, what is to come could be a doorway to an even greater experience.

Everything you are seeking to find fulfillment in is only a matter of seeking within yourself. From this view, attainment becomes unlimited.

#TheUniverseLovesYou

The Art Of Having

**"There are no ends or beginnings.
There is just a constant flow of universal
ABUNDANCE and you are in the midst of it
all."**
Roxana Jones

There's a powerful way to possess all that we desire, available to each and every one of us that exists right now at this moment. It's called the process of having, or the art of having. The universe leaves clues for us to live the life that makes us the happiest.

One of the greatest methods to receiving all that you choose is "feeling from the end result."

When we think about all of the things we are attempting to manifest for ourselves, they all have one thing in common. They all are just states of feeling and being. That's right! It's not about the car, or the house, or the big bank balance. It is all about the feelings within that these objects create.

The most wonderful thing is, you can bypass the object and go straight to the feeling. If you've ever reached the goal of having a new car then you know exactly what that feels like. If it's not as clear as you'd like it to be, close your eyes and ask yourself the question, "What does it feel like to have a brand new car? What feeling does this desire bring you?"

Behind every desire is a feeling that you are longing to feel. The more you can feel this feeling now, the faster you can manifest your desire. The car provides freedom to travel where you would like to go. What else does the car provide for you? What areas of your life do you have freedom right now? Do you have the freedom to travel? Do you have the freedom to be you? Freedom to choose the foods you eat, the activities you do? Feel all the ways that you are free and the more you feel free and blessed the more freedom is given to you.

If you are desiring a loving relationship, notice in your life where you are experiencing love, intimacy, nurturing, and comfort. Focus on the feelings of your desire that you already experience in your life. As you feel the freedom, joy, love, success now at this moment and all throughout the day, the faster you bring your desires into your life. As you bathe in gratitude for all that you have, more reasons to be grateful come into your life.

Your subconscious mind is wired to seek out and find the answer to every question the conscious mind asks, it will offer you the exact feeling in no time. The same goes for manifesting money in your life. **It's not the actual money we desire, it's the feeling of freedom, joy and security of being taken care of. That's where we have to place our focus.**

So when you decide that it is more money you choose to have, focus upon the feeling of freedom, safety, joy, and security. Ask yourself with clarity what the exact feeling feels like? What does the freedom, joy, and security of having $20,000 in monthly income feel like to take care of my needs and desires?

Getting into the feeling state of abundance is essential to bring your desires more easily and joyfully to you. Think about the top three desires you wish for right now in your life. Is it to buy your dream car or house, get married to a loving partner, start a successful business doing what you love? Think about everything you desire, that keeps you up at night fantasizing about it.

The feeling produces the end result. This means that the benevolent universe is forever responding to the feelings that we are putting out via our thoughts, thought patterns, and feelings. Each moment of every day, universal law responds depending upon the magnitude of the feeling. This creates a significant revelation for us all when it comes to living the life that we truly desire.

We must feel into the life that we desire first, to allow it to enter our consciousness. Once it has entered our consciousness, the manifestation will be automatic.

Give it a moment to sink in and use your mind to zero in on that feeling. Something magical will occur when we do so, and that magic is called the state of having. The longer we can hold this state of having, the faster it will enter our existence as an extended feeling, synchronistic event, or manifestation of the thing desired.

Finding Clarity

Before we can get into the state of having, there exists a very important task to complete. We must discover clarity in all that we desire. This is an absolute must for the universe to function optimally on our behalf. It's important because universal law works with incredible precision and accuracy.

It encourages us to be as concise as we would when selecting anything of great importance in our lives. With that being said, another question to ask and ask frequently is, "What do I truly desire to have in my life?"

Before we answer this in its entirety, we must understand that it is not "things" that we ultimately wish to have, but feelings and states of being. Once we're clear on the emotions we are desiring to feel, we can create an intention for the universe to bring an unlimited amount of that feeling.

The beauty is that, just by asking for the feeling, you will receive a multitude of circumstances that will create the same feeling.

When we live from a state of trust and having, the universe can more easily bless us with what we desire. The state of having is coming from a place of abundance. You are focusing on what you have versus what you are lacking.

Thoughts of abundance bring more abundance into your life. Thoughts of lack bring more experiences of lack. Know that you already have everything you need. You have enough food to eat, you have enough clothes to wear, you have enough of everything. When you live in a state of having, you open the doors to having more.

You can step into this abundance consciousness of the universe when you let go and believe that it is already yours. It all starts with feeling gratitude for your life now. Step into the feeling of how wonderful your life is now. Think about how rich you are now with love, experiences, opportunities, relationships, and where you live. Feel into all of this as much as possible. The feeling produces the end result.

As you feel it now, you open up a golden doorway for the universe to give you more of what you feel.

When you think of unconditional love and support, no one or nothing has your back like the universe. Move from the heart's desires and the success will inevitably be yours.

#TheUniverseLovesYou

Your Heart's Desire

**"Whatever God puts in your heart, He
gives the power to accomplish it."
Lailah Gifty Akita**

Have you ever wondered why you choose the
goals, dreams, desires, and aspirations you
do? Have you ever sat down and probed the
curiosity as to why you've chosen to have
something? This is an all-important question
we must look into whenever we are desiring to
have something in our lives. If by some
chance, you find yourself in a situation where
the desire for it feels authentic and oftentimes
unexplainable, then you are on to something
of great magnitude.

The universe places within us all, a true heart's
desire. Within the scope of this desire is
everything needed to realize it into
manifestation. This is one of the most
eminent ways to truly discover if something is
meant for you. Has there been a high level of
difficulty in achieving it? Have you

encountered one obstacle after another? Are you doing it because it pays well? Do you feel drawn to it? Does it bring you more energy and excitement?

By answering these questions you peel away the layers of your heart's desire and find true fulfillment. The more layers you can strip away, the more clarity you can experience in discovering the Divinely designed truth for life.

When you follow your heart's desire, that which brings you infinite joy, you benefit from the universe's kindness, love, and generosity.

The universe gives us everything we could possibly need to find out the truth behind our desires. It wants to see us successful, as well as, see us continue to evolve throughout our journey.

We were all created for a definite, unique, distinguishable purpose to bring forth into this world. With that purpose came numerous talents and gifts to aid in its development. If we look back over the course of our lives, we can watch as these gifts and talents have been brought about into our existence.

Once we've locked into what this purpose is, the universe stops at nothing to make it a reality because it's not only you that's benefitting from it all, but so many others. Sometimes even on a global scale. The universe does this because self-actualization and love are its guiding principles throughout the entire cosmos.

There is one particular way that we can know for sure that we have unveiled this purpose, our heart's true desire. It feels similar to an invisible hand guiding you along with your life, taking care of you, watching out for you, correcting your course when you stray, and offering you signs as well as inner guidance to choose the highest path.

Can you specifically say to yourself, "I already know what this purpose is?" If so, congratulations. If not, no need to worry. Because you're reading this book, you are following your highest path.

Uncover Your Heart's Desire

All you have to do is ask the question with a heartfelt feeling of care and compassion behind your question, "What is my heart's truest desire that the universe has selected for me to bring forth in this life?"

Take some time with this profound question. It's a great idea to meditate on this question, get into a relaxed state and ask. Even if you don't receive an answer right away, it's completely fine. What will unfold is signs because your consciousness is now aligned with what the universe truly desires for you. All we have to do is ask, and we shall receive because we are truly and unconditionally loved by the benevolent universe.

To find out if a desire is truly from your heart, ask yourself these questions, "Does it make me a better person? Does it benefit those around me? Does it enable me to grow more into my Divine purpose? Does it make me happy?" If you have answered yes to all these questions, then you are on the right track to uncovering your heart's desire from the universe.

The greatest discovery is the search for the complete wholeness of ourselves. This is the journey that carries all of life's solutions.

#TheUniverseLovesYou

Needing Nothing Attr. Everything

When we have faith in our desires and we let them go, the universe can deliver.

The Universe adores you and wants to shower you will all the love, abundance, and blessings you deserve. This loving source wants to provide you everything that enriches your life. Everything you want from your heart the universe wants for you. Isn't that a liberating feeling to know that your dreams, wishes, and desires are also the dreams of the universe?

At the beginning of time, the universe made an invaluable promise to provide abundantly for every living thing within it. This generosity is rooted in the unconditional love that is present in every moment that exists. The universe only knows love, it only knows giving. Anything that conflicts with this is only a lack of a universal perception.

Nature is abundantly supplied with everything to keep it thriving, plentiful, and sustainable. There is never, under any circumstance, any presence of lack anywhere in nature. Even the appearance of lack, such as a barren tree during winter, still carries the essence of abundance and life force energy within it.

The universe works through balance and at the root of that balance is an inexhaustible source. This source is the foundation of everything you see in nature, even when it appears to be invisible the absence is still present in either the form of substance or the form of energy.

The sun is one of the greatest sources of abundance that the universe offers. It generously gives its radiant light to promote endless growth and vibrancy to everything on the planet. The sun offers its warmth and nourishment for expansion to all living things. This is the result because of the universe's love for nature.

Just imagine if the universe gives this freely to nature, how much more does the universe want to equally bless you?

So you might ask, "Why do I not have what I desire? Why am I struggling with my relationships, finances, or happiness?" The problem lies in our mistrust of life, ourselves, the universe, God. We have been taught that we need to force things to happen, we need to control things to go our way. This puts us into a state of resistance. The more we resist, the more we block and sabotage all the support, abundance, and blessings from the universe.

This perception that you have to do it all yourself is misguided. The idea that you have to push, force, and manipulate everything to work for you is where the damaging belief stems from. The universe adores you so much that it doesn't want you to have to struggle, sabotage yourself yet again and get in your own way. But that is exactly the problem, we are really good at getting in our own way.

The desire of always needing to be, do and have more blocks the universal flow of enjoying what you already have right now. Needing something is a state of lack because it signifies not only do you not have what you are desiring, you are in a constant state of wanting, which continually drives it away from you.

You won't ever get something when you are in a state of needing it because mentally and emotionally you don't have it within.

"Needing nothing attracts everything."
Russell Simmons.

Imagine being in a relationship where one person is constantly needing attention from the other person. This need for attention comes from never having enough, the energy becomes overbearing and pushes the other person away.

To need nothing and attract everything you desire, it starts with expressing gratitude for everything you already have in your life right now. Being grateful is a state of abundance that magnetizes more reasons to be grateful.

When you feel the deep emotion of gratitude it transforms the energy within yourself and your reality. Feel the wonderful feelings of appreciation in your heart and express them towards everything.

To need nothing means that you have a mental and emotional vision of the thing you desire within you. Simply put it's already yours within. For example, a vision board can be used to create a mental image of the thing you choose to have. Once we know what our desires look like within, it's easy for the universe to make them manifest for us, as long as we stay in a state of abundance and without attachment.

If you are struggling financially think of the feeling you get the moment you receive an amount of money that not only covers your needs but also gives you an even bigger surplus. Doesn't that feel like relief, comfort, peace? So, create that feeling first within you. Once you have a sense of relief and peace, you can settle in knowing that your desires are on their way to you.

Trust yourself, take the leap, and the universe will guide you. There is no worry, no pressure, no wrong way to go. Believe that your path is unfolding perfectly for you. Be patient the journey will last as long as it needs to, when you reach your destination you will become the person you came here to become.

Within each moment lies the perfection of every breath you take, every sunset you've encountered, and every smile you gave to others. With all these blessings present within you, you are already on the path of needing nothing and attracting everything.

Instead of focusing on what you need more of, focus on what you are already are blessed with and more will be given to you.

#TheUniverseLovesYou

Your Superpower Of Gratitude

"Through the eyes of gratitude, everything is a miracle."
Mary Davis

There is one sure-fire way to transform your life into one of overflowing joy, peace, and happiness. This method is gratitude, your universal superpower. This one state of mind and being can alter the course of your life extraordinarily all for your benefit. It is also one of the simplest mindsets to practice because, right now, there are endless opportunities surrounding you to be grateful.

For years Sarah sequestered the universe to bring her financial riches. The whole while she honestly thought that nothing was unfolding for her. Then one day as she was spending her daily hour in the forest, she began to see how rich she had been all along her entire life. The universe directed her to recount all of the money she had received since she had been born. She was completely blown away by all the financial blessings that she received.

Surprisingly enough, the first number she came up with wasn't truly accurate because she left out all of the money her parents circulated for her throughout her mom's pregnancy and the first few years of her life. She could only consciously remember back since the age of five, so there was so much more that was present for her benefit.

The gratitude she experienced brought her to tears. She also began to think about the third-world countries she was so fortunate to visit that starkly reminded me of the pleasure-filled life she had been blessed to experience. All she could say was, "Universe thank you so very much for answering my prayer even before I had asked. You have enabled me to be my happiest and most fulfilled."

This is such an important message to convey, mainly because we usually have the very thing we are asking the universe for, and gratitude is the power that reveals the truth of its existence. From that day forward, she used every waking opportunity to count the endless blessings she had every day. It was ultimately the smaller, more noticeable things that have created the greatest impact. She learned the timeless truth that happiness really is an inside job. If we're missing the mark, we just have to be pointed in the right direction.

We must ponder the statement, "Universe allow me to see with clarity and knowing the blessings in my life that I can express my most sincere heartfelt gratitude."

This opens the mind to the idea that will flood your life with opportunities that have gone unnoticed. Think about how grateful you are for your health, specifically your heart beating, your lungs processing oxygen, and your cells working in unison. Think about how grateful you are to walk from your home to anywhere you want to go. Appreciate the value of having legs that are healthy enough to get you there. Express gratitude for the clothes that keep you warm and the shoes that protect your feet.

Think about your relationships and how they have blessed your life. Although you might not always agree on things, you can always agree on love and well-being for each other. This is something to be grateful for. Think of all the memories you have shared and the love you have felt.

Feel the outpouring of gratitude you have that is present in your life. Never take anything in life for granted, but welcome all of it in immense gratitude.

You deserve to be grateful in your life because you deserve to live a life that brings you happiness, joy, and fulfillment. Even in the toughest of situations, what can you pull out of it that you can be grateful for? Is there anyone that you are having a hard time with? Feel gratitude for the fact that they are offering you the gift to learn how to love more. This could positively shift the nature of your relationship with this individual.

Gratitude enables us to always understand that which we have, as opposed to that which seems to be taken away. This especially comes in handy when it comes to money. How often have we consistently thought, if I just had more, if I just could get to this exact number, I'd be happy?

When in actuality, the simple act of appreciating what you already have summons forth the energy to manifest more in your life. Gratitude creates shifts of all kinds, including health, relationships, state of mind, emotional well-being, and spirituality.

Gratitude would almost be akin to wiping a dusty window to look outside and see the beauty it was covering. It truly makes everything clear and as it should be, something to be grateful for.

If you're having issues in any area, there's no reason to get overwhelmed by it. If you have pain in your body, use gratitude to transform it. Gratitude infuses the cells with the energy of healing. Being grateful possesses the power to see the blessing in all things.

The universe has granted you a superpower that can transform any situation into an abundance of happiness. You just have to attune to it, and you attune to it by making it a habit to always seek, love, and express gratitude in everything.

Gratitude has been given to us freely by the benevolent universe, it once again proves without any shadow of a doubt, the universe loves us unconditionally and desires us to experience the highest growth, good and potential that is available to us.

Gratitude Mindset

Gratitude is a way of life not just an activity we take part in when we think about it. It should be as significant as having a meal, taking a shower, or brushing our teeth. It deserves that type of importance because of its expansive magnitude.

Set a gratitude reminder on your phone to go off every hour. With each reminder focus on how grateful you are and fill your heart with love. This is a great way to learn to express more gratitude in your life. Focus on everything in gratitude from the small things to the more encompassing things. Gratitude is a way of life that blesses you greatly. Living in gratitude is a highly effective way to enhance your life.

**"The universe provides abundantly when you're in a state of gratefulness."
Wayne Dyer**

As you follow what you love to do, more opportunities, money, and people will come into your life to help you on your path. It's so powerful to wake up every day and do what you love and share your gifts with the world.

#TheUniverseLovesYou

Do What You Love

"If you follow your dreams and spend your life doing what brings you joy, you are more likely to find success."
Richard Branson

The universe knows, inherently, if we do what we feel the greatest affinity for, we will live abundantly happy lives. So much so that we can barely contain the excitement of getting out of bed in the morning. The universe really wants us to do what we love.

We can often lose sight of this truth at times because of challenging circumstances, but if we go into every life experience with the knowing that every single occurrence since the beginning of time is a blessing, we will, undoubtedly, thrive through anything. This gives us peace beyond understanding and relaxation that creates inevitable mindfulness.

For just a few moments, I'd like for you to think of someone that makes you smile or laugh heartily. Take your time as you do this and really focus on the person that makes you smile. Now, pay attention to what happens to your body. Your shoulders tend to relax, you might even get goosebumps, you experience joy and peace come over your body.

Just by doing this simple exercise, you have stepped into a state of love. It's important to remember this process because this is the exact thing you're going to do as it relates to doing what you love in life, which also turns out to be your purpose.

What Do You Love To Do?

Think about the very thing that you would do every single day that brings a smile to your face. Imagine not being paid for this thing not because there's lack, but because you're in a position to not have to be concerned about money. Would you still do it? If so, do you often find yourself being creative around this thing? Are you consistently finding ways to make it better and more effective? Is it something that makes you feel good inside because of the impact it creates on others?

These questions are all significant in finding what you love to do. But, they're even more significant because once you find the thing that you are here, on this earth to do, the universe will not just provide, but back you up in making sure that you have everything you need to succeed at it.

One profound aspect of this entire concept is, we often are unaware of what we love to do, but because the universe loves us unconditionally, it is forever guiding us towards it. It cares greatly when it comes to doing what you love regularly.

(Shaun) I remember growing up and I loved to sing. Sometimes I would be so off-key that I would often laugh at myself when I missed a note. I loved the entire process and I still do to this day. But, there was a time when singing, something I truly loved doing that made me feel so good inside, wasn't fun anymore. That is the only element that matters when it comes to doing what you love, fun. It became more about taking lessons, finding a manager, a label, and a bunch of other things that took me on the scale of joy from 100 to 3.

I learned something irreplaceably valuable during that time, if you're doing something to get something in return, it's not really love, but the desired outcome you want to benefit from instead. Just to be clear, I'm not saying you can't be paid, because you can be paid extraordinarily well for what you love.

It's more or less placing your primary focus on attaining something. Long story short, I stopped singing altogether. If I couldn't do it at the vibration of love, then it wasn't for me. It wasn't until I heard my favorite song from a long time ago, that I broke my years-long hiatus. Instantly, all of the initial joy came rushing back!

I made a promise to myself from that day forward. I always wanted to do the things that I loved because that made my life feel its best. If I was to be paid, it would be off the energy that I gave through the channel of the thing I loved doing. The universe, since that day, has continued to reward me for giving my gifts, and more importantly, following its lead and doing what I love to do.

As you follow what you love to do, more opportunities, money, and people will come into your life to help you on your path. It's so powerful to wake up every day and do what you love and share your gifts with the world. Not only does it benefit you and your happiness, well-being, but it benefits the whole world.

Listen To Your Heart

Your heart is guiding your highest fulfillment and happiness, all you have to do is listen. Instead of doing what everyone else is doing, follow what leads to the most joy for you.

Don't google what you should do, instead, listen to the wisdom of your heart to live the life of your dreams. Follow the love of what speaks to your heart.

By having the courage to do what you love and what brings you the most joy, you will receive the most fulfillment. Be willing to listen to your heart and walk on your own path even when it's a different path to others. Listen to your intuition and express your creative urges and this will unfold an incredible journey of your soul.

Believe in yourself, listen to your heart, and do what you love.

Make happiness your highest priority.

#TheUniverseLovesYou

Your Universal Gift To Be Happy

"Happiness radiates like the fragrance from a flower and draws all good things towards you."
Maharishi Mahesh Yogi

Happiness is your birthright, the universe wants you to be happy. It is a choice that you have to make every moment of the day. It's up to you to align with the happiness that is always available. The universe gives you endless opportunities to be happy every morning you wake up, but it's up to you to choose happiness. The universe offers a whole array of pleasures at the moment, but you have to be present.

Do you feel happy when you wake up from a peaceful night's rest? Happiness lies in the feeling of gratitude to see another day. Happiness comes from being present and breathing deeply. Happiness is knowing that every part of your body can function properly without any hindrances. Happiness comes in the simple moments of observing the beauty of nature, watching a sunrise, sitting on the ocean's edge, or walking in the forest.

Happiness is a feeling of peace, joy, and tranquility at the moment as it is. Happiness is not contingent on outside circumstances but a choice you make inside yourself no matter what is happening around you. Happiness is something that can not be given or taken away, it's a choice you make within. The universe offers all that you need to choose to be happy.

You have a mind to think happy thoughts, a heart to feel happy feelings, and the ability to combined both thoughts and feelings to create a state of happiness. There is never a time when this choice isn't there. Happiness is about perspective.

Imagine losing your job, at first glance, this would be a cause unhappiness. What if this was an opportunity to have more of your time, do more of what you love, and eventually make more money? This would be a reason to be extremely happy. In this example, we can see that happiness is a choice and it all depends on how you perceive things. Your attitude is everything when it comes to happiness.

Happiness is a shift in your thinking process, when you realize that you can be happy now versus always waiting for things to make you happy. Another paradox of life is most people believe that happiness is found in things, events, or other people, but it's actually found in the everyday workings of our hearts and minds. This shift easily and effortlessly creates a life that can bring you endless joy.

Instead of choosing fame, success, and money as your highest priority, make happiness your highest priority. Make choices based on how happy it makes you. At the end of the day, being happy first will bring all those things to you as a byproduct of your happiness.

**"Happiness comes from within you. You'll
never find it by chasing relationships, jobs,
beauty, money. Happiness always starts
within."**
Anonymous

Happiness In The Moment

In each moment, the universe is blessing you
with a life full of love, happiness,
opportunities, and new adventures. Stop for a
moment and focus on what the universe is
giving you all the time. Your greatest gifts are
found in the present moment. Move away
from always needing something else and allow
the universe to give to you.

In the now you are always being blessed with
new insights, ideas, and wisdom to help you
on your journey for the greatest fulfillment.
Open up to the present moment and be
blessed every day.

Love is the most empowering force in the universe. To experience your ideal life, it's essential to follow the universe's path to loving yourself. Loving yourself embodies self-acceptance, self-appreciation and self-confidence.

#TheUniverseLovesYou

Your Universal Gift To Love And Be In Love

Follow your universal guidance system, guiding you with emotions, intuition, and how you are feeling. As you pay attention to what feels the best, you are on the inevitable path to true love.

The universe offers every one of us the distinct opportunity to be in love and live in love. There is a catch to this and the only way to find true love is to love yourself first.

Unconditional love is one of the universe's primary objectives. Unconditional love is to love freely, is full acceptance of all that is and all that we are. It's a Divine attribute that is given freely to enjoy and express.

The most important way to maximize this love in your life is through Divine connection to all that is, to God. We have to choose to take as many moments as possible to embody our Divine self. When the Divine self is embodied unconditional love floods our being as well as our life. The presence of the Divine self also makes us attractive to others.

The universe encourages you to feel, express, and act with a heart of love. The more love that you share with others the more love that returns back to you.

To find the ideal mate, it's essential to follow the universe's path to loving yourself. Loving yourself is self-acceptance, self-appreciation and self-confidence.

Self-acceptance starts with taking responsibility for everything good and bad that has happened in your life and still knowing within that you are worthy of love.

Self-appreciation is being grateful for those experiences that have shaped you into who you are and their ability to teach you how to love.

Self-confidence is having the ability to know that you, coupled with all your experiences, are worthy of love. Although this doesn't have to be perfect in practice, it's the intention to love oneself that matters the most.

As your self-love and acceptance grows the better your relationships are. Once the universe feels like the love for self is adequate the opportunity for your ideal mate to come into your life will show up. Self-love teaches you how to make optimal decisions that serve the growth and well-being of your relationship.

The Guiding Light Of Love

Much like a compass, the universe is guiding us in a direction that offers love, bliss, and harmony for both people involved. When it comes to love the universe always encourages inclusion because it wants you to think about how everything you do affects your partner. From a universal perspective, when we make decisions that serve the well-being of ourselves and our partner we enhance the quality of our relationship.

The universe is our guidance system which shows us if we are in a relationship that serves our highest good. All you need to do is check-in with how you are feeling on a predominant basis, love or the opposite of love.

What you say about the person to your friends and family is a good indicator of how you really feel about your partner. Any red flags or warning signs will be revealed to you. Refuse to be attached to anyone, if you are feeling lonely or desperate. The universe wants to bring you the right person to excel in your growth and happiness.

The universe wants you to be happily in love and it's willing to offer every advantage needed to enable that to manifest. It loves you, it supports you, and its greatest desire is to see you living the life of your dreams filled with peace, love, and abundance.

"Abundance is a mindset. It's a way of thinking, a state of mind. It's a state of being, rather than a state of doing."

Sallie Keys

Your Universal Gift To Be Abundant

"The universe is a source of unlimited supply. It is enough for everyone. If we focus on abundance, our feelings, emotions, and actions eventually attract abundance into our lives."
Bob Proctor

Money is an expression of the universe that is backed by the energy of love. Its primary purpose when used correctly is to do as much good in your own life, as well as the lives of others. Seeing money in a negative light hinders it from flowing freely into your life.

There is another reason why money is so important that we lose sight of it, and it has to do with one of the universe's primary objectives. Every amount of money that has ever come into our lives correlates to our growth and self-actualization.

In the economy we live in today, it would be difficult to live your life in a way that the universe desires for you without having enough money. We become who we are destined to be and the universe utilizes the money to play a big part in that.

The universe created money to be a simple concept. As within, so without is the first truth about money. The reason being money is completely reflective of our thoughts and feelings. God has created a centralized universal mind that takes the dominant thoughts and feelings of every individual on the planet and moves them into physical manifestation in perfect harmony with the universe.

So if you look at your life right now, you can observe what thoughts and feelings you are focusing on the most by the amount of money you have in your life. If you have lots of money, your thoughts and feelings are resonating with the abundance of the universe. If you are lacking in money, there is no need to worry, you just have to focus on your thoughts on the abundance of the universe. By holding thoughts and feelings for an extended period of time, this expedites the manifestation of those thoughts and feelings. Hence more money flowing into your life.

God wants you to have more than enough free of worry and struggle. This is your Divine birthright and all you have to do is align with the universe's objectives of self-actualization and especially love. God desires more than anything to give you all that you need and desire to live a happy, fulfilled life.

Embrace Your Riches

Focus on the truth that all the money you would ever need and desire for your life is available to you now. Not only is it available to you, but it is destined to show up at the perfect Divine time.

Take as long as you need to embrace wholeheartedly this truth and pay attention to how it shifts the way of being. What does this feel like? For some it's relief. For some it's freedom. For others it's peace. Whichever one resonates with you, remember how it feels because this is the state that creates more abundance in your life.

Every time we access the state of abundance within ourselves it will always be through a calm, relaxing, and tranquil existence. If we observe the universe in action around us, one of the first things we notice is that it does everything with ease. It is the same easiness that offers you the greatest avenue to prosper when it comes to money or any form of abundance.

In order to truly maximize the abundance in your life choose to reside in stillness and calm as much as you can. When you are at ease, the universe can move into action and manifest your abundance right before your eyes. It's a simple process that balances action with stillness.

A way to understand receiving from the universe can be found in the example of driving a car. When driving, you never put your foot on the brake and gas at the same time. Each one is done separately as the need arises. In this case, the gas represents action and the brake represents stillness.

Imagine the universe as a traffic light and you are driving in a car on route to a destination. As the universe turns to green, you step on the gas peddle and this is the universe's way of informing you to safely move forward. When the universe turns red and you push the brake, this is its way of informing you to be still.

This demonstrates the perfect dynamic when it comes to receiving from the universe to achieve our goal. When it leads us to act we move forward by pressing the gas and when it leads us to be still we embrace stillness by pressing the brake. In both of these actions, we eventually reach our Divinely designed destination.

Gaze up at the sun and
feel how loved you are.
You are so loved by the
sky, clouds, trees, plants,
flowers, and birds. You
are so loved by mother
earth.

#TheUniverseLovesYou

The Universe Loves You

**The universe is always blessing you
every moment of the day.**

The universe truly adores you. Look up at the
sun and see how loved you are. You are so loved
by the sky, clouds, trees, plants, flowers, and
birds. You are so loved by mother earth. Bathe
in this love like a big warm loving hug all day
long.

**As you walk outside, feel the love the
universe has for you. As you work, feel the
love the universe has for you. As you go
about your day, feel the love the universe has
for you.**

The universe loves you so much that it nourishes
you, supports you, heals you, blesses you with
loving relationships and a healthy body. The
universe gives you the wisdom, insight, and
understanding to be the person you came here
to be.

The universe loves you so much that it provides for you, offers you experiences of growth and introspection, experiences of love, and gives you the courage to follow your dreams. The universe blesses you with your creativity and imagination.

The truth is, the universe loves you unconditionally that without hesitation it gave you its very own Divinely dynamic power to create the life you choose. It is filled with such compassion and kindness, that it has desired to aid and comfort you through every hardship and struggle you have faced up to this point.

Feel The Love The Universe Has For You

Take as long as you need to feel into this statement. Allow it to sink into your being and focus on the feeling it creates.

"The universe loves me unconditionally. The universe loves me unconditionally. The universe loves me unconditionally."

What does that feel like? Do you feel safe? Do you feel secure? Do you feel loved? Do you feel overwhelmed with joy? As you continue to focus on that statement alone by itself, a powerful thing is occurring within your very being.

The universe's true essence of love, kindness, and compassion is permeating your consciousness. You begin to think from this place of being, feel from this place of being, and eventually act from this place of being. Every act you partake in is governed by the truth and promise of unconditional universal love.

Once we've accepted and understood intently that our consciousness is what creates our reality, we will begin to shift our focus to all the things that serve us as opposed to hinder us. We will decidedly, seek joy in everything and everyone.

We place our ability to succeed and be fulfilled on automatic. To be guided by universal love is likened much to the idea that Ralph Waldo Emerson proposed, "God's dice are always loaded." We've interpreted this in our own lives to be this simple yet effectively powerful truth in every way:

The universe loves me unconditionally and works everything, absolutely everything out in my favor. All I must do is adopt its highest objectives into my consciousness, and that will be my reality.

Reaffirm The Universe's Love For You And Your Trust Within It

I can relax into the arms of the universe and know everything will be okay. The universe supports me every day, and in everything I do.

Every breath I take I am loved and encouraged to be the very best version of myself. The more I relax and let go, the more I can attune to the universe's generosity. I am so greatly cherished and taken care of. All my needs are met and so much more.

With gratitude in my heart, I am completely fulfilled and free to be my authentic self. Gratitude is a state of being that I choose all throughout my day. The more open I am to universal flow, the happier my life is.

The universe supports me.
The universe loves me.
The air nourishes me.
The sun bathes me in unconditional rays of light.
The water hydrates me.
The rain replenishes me.
The wind cools me.
The moon enlightens me.
The plants nurture me.
The universe provides me a place to rest my head.
The universe embraces me in love.
The universe bathes me in love.
With all the overflowing love and support that I get every day, I trust the universe.
The universe loves to take care of me.
The universe adores me.
I feel safe and trust the universe.
I am well taken care of.
Everything is working out the best for me when I let go and trust the universe.
The universe guides me on my journey.
I can relax and feel calm, the universe is always loving and supporting me.
I always have enough.
I have more than enough.
I am nurtured.

I am loved.
I am fully supported.
The universe created me to be all that I need.
The universe showers me with unconditional love and tender loving care.
I am walking my path knowing that I am completely loved and supported.
I am feeling whole, complete, and enough.
I am a marvelous creation of the universe, being all that I can be in every moment that is gifted to me.
All the energies of the universe are working in cohesion with my deepest feelings, thoughts, and beliefs.
My soul's connection creates endless happiness and fulfillment.
The universe is always blessing me.
The universe loves and supports me every moment of the day.

"Within each of us is a Divine universe of love."

Dr. Debra Reble

Living In Universal Love

"Love is the very foundation, beauty, and fulfillment of life. If we dive deep enough into ourselves, we will find that one thread of universal love ties all beings together. As this awareness draws within us, peace alone will reign."
Mata Amritanandamayi

There are no coincidences in life, nothing happens by chance, everything is synchronized to the rhythm of the universe to manifest on purpose. Every person contains the whole universe within themselves. We are all expressions of the universe and we are aligned together in this concept of oneness through universal love.

As we let go of our limiting beliefs and everything that doesn't serve us, the universe can function optimally to bring our highest good. Much like releasing judgment, when we say goodbye to all lower vibrational energies, we can experience the unconditional love the universe so willingly wants to give us.

To fully be present and experience the joy of life the universe offers, it's essential to feel a deep relaxation and peace with life. By letting go of our fears and worries and surrendering to complete trust we open to unlimited possibilities.

As we dive deep within ourselves through silent time and meditation, we can connect to the heart of the universe. **At the core of your being, your soul guided by the universe is loving and supporting you on your journey. By going within and focusing on the essence of your soul you tap into your unlimited power, wisdom, and unconditional love that is always present in your life.**

The universe is always guiding you with loving wisdom to give you insight into all you need to know. All you have to do is ask and listen for the answers you are seeking. Not only what feels good, but also what feels like ease and reassurance is your intuition leading you down your highest path. Keep your heart open to always be in alignment with your universal blessings.

With love all things are possible. Know with certainty and faith that everything is working out the best for you. Even if you can't see it at the moment, everything is being orchestrated in your favor behind the scenes. The now, also known as the present, is all there is. If you keep your attention focused at the moment a beautiful thing unfolds. You realize that you have always had exactly what you need. The present moment always gives to us the greatest joy and abundance.

The universe has supplied your greatest form of happiness in the things you love to be and do. By discovering the things you love most authentically, you find the key to living your life you choose. Follow the trail that leads to joy because joy is one of the universe's most fulfilling gifts.

We manifest in direct correlation to our vibration. Our vibration is the sum total of all our most dominant thoughts, feelings, and beliefs that make up our energy field. It rises in frequency when we let go of all things that are heavy in nature and embrace the lightness that is the Divine essence.

You can raise your vibration by simply focusing on what makes you feel good. By holding this feeling for an extended period of time, what will occur is everything that is not in congruence with feeling good will rise to the surface to be released.

You are always self-actualizing as the universe expresses itself through you. Every moment of your life is dedicated to you reaching your highest potential of self-actualization. By attuning to universal love, self-actualization becomes an easier task to tap into. It's available every moment of each day.

Universal love is the pillar of our existence. Everything we have ever done since the beginning of time has been expressed through universal love. It is in every atom, molecule and makes up your very nature.

When used to help ourselves and humanity it becomes the most powerful source in the universe. This has been done on purpose for us to realize that we are on this earth to be loved and supported unconditionally.

Universal love has the best interest of everything and everyone contained within it. It is unconditionally serving this objective, as it continues to expand upon itself.

Universal love is in you, around you, and working through you. It craves interaction with you. Embrace this eternal gift that has been bestowed upon your life. Use universal love to take your life to the highest, best and happiest level possible.

If you knew that everything you ever wanted or desired was 100% going to show up in your life at the perfect moment, how would you live your life?

#TheUniverseLovesYou

Open To Receive All That Is Yours

"When faced with any life test, tell yourself this: If it works out, great. If it doesn't, even better. You know that your world takes care of you and so if something has not worked out, it means that you have avoided other problems you can't yet see."
Vadim Zeland

If you knew that everything you ever wanted or desired was 100% going to show up in your life at the perfect moment, how would you live your life? Wouldn't that take all the pressure off and allow you to enjoy your life so much more?

Take a long heartfelt moment to feel into this life-transforming truth. A truth that allows us to know without hesitation, that the universe plans to give you absolutely everything that contributes to you living your greatest life possible.

The universe is willing to hold nothing back because its very nature is to find every possibility to offer us our heart's desire. Our part in this Divinely orchestrated beauty is getting into alignment with its highest principles of self-actualization and unconditional love to receive all its blessings. From there we inevitably discover new areas of awareness that lead us right down the perfect path to fulfillment.

At this moment know with all your heart, nothing can stand in the way of getting what your heart chooses to have. Everything and we mean everything, has been set up just for you. Even when it seems like there is struggle or resistance, stop for just a moment and allow universal peace to fill you up. Peace permits all wisdom, insight, and understanding to come to the forefront to see the truth of any situation.

Most importantly, through any situation that arises, if you are unable to understand anything else, understand that the universe is loving, supporting, and there is nothing to ever fear, stress, or worry about.

The universe has and will continue to bless you more than you can imagine. Have you noticed in life, when things have worked out better than expected? Your commitment to the universe's guidance and wisdom, profits you in abundant ways with everything you partake in. This is your reward and ultimately a surprise from the universe.

The Bible states that perfect love casts out all fear. The universe's love is perfect and not only does it transmute fear, but anything else that stands in the way of you embodying all of your dynamic soul qualities while realizing your highest soul potential.

Realizing your highest soul potential is your birthright. It is your eternal calling. It is your soul-song.

Know this, feel this, embrace this, love this, and your life will unfold in a perfect way to prove what you now realize, has always been the truth. **The universe loves and supports you, always!**

About The Authors

Shaun Grant

Shaun Grant is a dynamic spiritual entrepreneur who was born and raised in the heart of New Orleans, Louisiana. Shaun learned the power of resiliency which allowed him to grow into an individual who is forever led by kindness, love, and compassion in all that he does.

Shaun produces life-enhancing content that enables people to actualize their authentic selves. He also devotes time to counseling others on how to successfully navigate prosperity, abundance, and money. His methods have been effective in enlightening people on what it takes to manifest a healthy, vibrant, and sustaining relationship with their finances. His book, ***The Money Cure: Healing Your Relationship To Money And Discovering The True Path To Abundance,*** powerfully expands the concept of being rich and feeling peace with money.

He teaches that a relationship with the Divine within is the most significant part of living a life that is perfect for the mind, body, and soul. By placing the soul's directives first, it becomes inevitable that only the most fulfilling things will unfold in everyone's life. Connect with Shaun on Instagram @Iamshaungrant / Facebook @shaungrant / Youtube @shaungrant

Sarah Grant

Sarah Grant is the author of ***Soul Beauty and Sacred Self Love And Body Confidence.*** As a highly sought after coach, she designs customized programs for nutrition, transformation, and emotional healing. Sarah helps people to navigate their personal path to health, happiness, and wholeness. She teaches specialized methods on how to love yourself, live a soul-centered life, and discover the bliss and ease within you.

Sarah lives in South Florida with her husband, Shaun Grant, and loves spending time outdoors, meditating, and connecting with the beauty of life. She loves traveling the world and learning about the spirituality, ancient healing practices, and beauty habits of different cultures.

Sarah offers guided meditations and affirmations, online courses, and coaching programs. Visit Sarah's website at www.theSarahGrant.com for more of her work and how to work with her one on one. Connect with her on Instagram @thesarahgrant / Facebook @Iamsarahgrant

Books by Sarah Grant

Soul Beauty: Awaken The Love, Light & Bliss Within You

Sacred Self Love And Body Confidence: Love Yourself, Feel Confident And Get Rid Of Your Inner Critic For Good

Affirmation tracks available on all music outlets (iTunes, Spotify, Amazon)

Goddess Affirmations: Embrace Your Wholeness And Connect To Your Inner Bliss

Abundance Affirmations: Listen, Speak And Feel Your Way To Abundance

Gratitude Affirmations: Improve Your Life, Increase Your Abundance And Feel Your Best

Color Healing Meditation: Bathe Yourself In The Healing Colors Of The Rainbow

Books by Shaun Grant

The Money Cure: Healing Your Relationship To Money And Discovering The True Path To Abundance

The Vibrational Actor: A Heart-Centered Approach To Acting

Become A Powerhouse In Auditioning: An Actor's Guide To Top Level Auditioning

Affirmation tracks available on all music outlets (iTunes, Spotify, Amazon)

Energize Your Love: Inspirational Audio

Made in United States
North Haven, CT
11 April 2022